W9-AJL-929

Forgiveness

Max Malikow

Forgiveness

Note: Unless otherwise indicated, biblical quotations in this book are from the New International Version translation of the Holy Bible.

ISBN 9781737264514

Preface

Since there are literally hundreds of books on forgiveness, it's reasonable to ask, "Why one more?" This is an especially relevant question since this book offers nothing new on the subject. Its purpose resides in for whom it is written. Long ago I gave up on the dream of writing a bestseller that would be financially rewarding and make me as well-known as Phil McGraw or Scott Peck. Since abandoning this dream I have cheerfully written for my students and patients, who benefit from having a professor and therapist respectively who has organized his thoughts and scrutinized his beliefs. Serious writing demands this of a writer.

I also write because, like George Orwell, not to write would go against my nature. Moreover, writing is the only hard work I enjoy and not to write would deprive me of a great pleasure. And so I write.

Max Malikow
Syracuse, NY
May 21, 2021

Introduction

Is forgiveness important? Could a relationship without forgiveness be sustained? (Jesus implied it would be intolerable and the only ground for divorce.) Is it possible for one nation to forgive another? Have the Japanese forgiven the United States for the atomic bombings of Hiroshima and Nagasaki? If so, how is international forgiveness expressed? Has the Jewish community forgiven the people of Germany for the Holocaust? Is it reasonable to ask people who did not participate in a "crime against humanity" to seek forgiveness? While these words are being written the United States House of Representatives is considering HR-40, a bill that would provide compensation to the descendants of slaves. If passed, would this constitute an adequate apology and would acceptance of the money signify forgiveness?

What if the idea of forgiveness didn't exist? What state of mind would fill the existing void? Revenge? Retribution? Resentment? Rage? The absence of forgiveness would obliterate the Christian faith to be sure. Would the world be a better place sans forgiveness as an option to the injured, offended or betrayed? Is forgiveness a virtue? If so, can a person be morally upright while withholding forgiveness? Finally, is a person who refuses to grant forgiveness forfeiting eligibility for receiving it?

This book is brief compared to numerous other books on forgiveness. Its brevity is intentional. Anyone deliberating on the possibility of forgiving someone is unlikely to benefit from a lengthy treatise on the subject. More likely to be helpful is an unambiguous analysis of what forgiveness is and is not along with an argument that favors forgiveness over withholding it.

Table of Contents

I. What Is Forgiveness?

Everyone says forgiveness is a lovely idea, until they have something to forgive.

- C.S. Lewis

Journalist Mike Barnicle writes:

> What is forgiveness? An emotion? A coping mechanism? An element of deepest faith? A way for the heart and soul to combat the type of hate, anger, rage, and thirst for revenge that could ultimately consume a person? All these and more (2021).

Philosopher Charles Griswald writes, "What is forgiveness? A moment's reflection reveals that forgiveness is a surprisingly complex and elusive notion. It is easier to say what it is not, than what it is" (2007, p. xiv). Fred Luskin, Director of Stanford University's Forgiveness Project, offers a list of what forgiveness is not:

> Forgiveness is not condoning unkindness.
> Forgiveness is not forgetting that something painful happened.
> Forgiveness is not excusing poor behavior.
> Forgiveness does not have to be an otherworldly or spiritual experience.
> Forgiveness is not denying or minimizing your hurt.

Forgiveness does not mean reconciling with the offender. Forgiveness does not mean you give up having feelings, including anger (2002, p. viii).

An extraordinary illustration of forgiveness is displayed in a letter written by Edgar Farrar, Sr. to the Governor of Louisiana. On November 1, 1911 in New Orleans Farrar's son, Edgar Farrar Jr., was murdered in broad daylight by a young burglar named Rene Canton. At trial Canton pleaded not guilty but the evidence against him was compelling and he was sentenced to death by hanging. Eight days before Canton's execution Edgar Farrar, Sr. made an appeal on behalf of his son's murderer. He asked the governor to commute Canton's sentence. Although the letter does not include the word forgive it encapsulates what forgiveness is and is not:

His Excellency, Luther E. Hall,
Governor of Louisiana,
Baton Rouge, LA.

Dear Sir:
On this day of Thanksgiving, the thoughts of all my household were turned to the chair made empty by the crime of the poor wretch, the date of whose execution you have fixed. This matter has been in our minds for some time, and after mature deliberation, all of us, father, mother, sisters, brothers and widow of my son,

have concluded to ask you to reprieve Rene Canton, and to send his case before the Board of Pardons for their consideration as to whether his sentence should not be commuted to imprisonment for life. We feel that this young brute is the product of our system of society, for which all of us, particularly persons of our position, are to some extent responsible. His father and mother are honest, hard working people. With them the struggle for existence was too bitter and exacting to permit them to devote the time and personal care necessary to develop the good and repress the evil in their son, who thus grew up amid the malign influences that surround the children of the poor in a large city. We believe that he shot my son as instinctively as a snake would strike one who crossed his path; and while his act was murder in law and in fact, yet it lacked that forethought and deliberation which make a crime of this sort unpardonable.

This man is now in no condition to be sent into the next world. We hope and pray that time and reflection will bring repentance and that his soul may be saved.

Your obedient servant,
Edgar Howard Farrar

On December 28, and with approval from the Board of Pardons, Governor Hall commuted Canton's death sentence to life imprisonment (1997, p. 403).

This letter shows an understanding of Rene Canton's criminal behavior without excusing it. It requests the consequences of his crime be altered, not eliminated. It expresses no wish for evil to befall him. To the contrary, it expresses a wish for his best, given his circumstances. And it conveys a family's compassion amidst inconsolable grief. This letter embodies philosopher Mike Martin's definition of forgiveness:

> Forgiveness is the act of relinquishing or avoiding negative attitudes toward someone for a wrong they have committed. Distinct from the outward act of telling others they are forgiven, forgiveness is an inner act or activity; it is a change of heart from ill will (hatred, anger, or contempt) to good will (1989, p. 91).

The example of forgiving a debt clarifies four conditions of forgiveness. One, the debt must actually exist even if the debtor refuses to acknowledge it. Two, forgiveness is given even if the debtor doesn't ask for forbearance. (More is said about this in the next chapter.) Third, the one to whom the debt is owed is under no obligation to forgive the debt. Four, forgiveness does not restore the debtor's eligibility to incur another debt from the forgiver.

II. The Forgiver

Forgiveness does not change the past, but it does enlarge the future.

- Paul Boese

Psychologist and Holocaust survivor Edith Eger writes of "the prison of not forgiving" in her memoir, *The Gift*:

> People often ask how I can ever forgive the Nazis. I don't have the godly power to anoint anyone with forgiveness, to spiritually cleanse others for their wrongs. But I have the power to free myself. So do you. Forgiveness isn't something we do for the person who's hurt us. It's something we do for ourselves, so we're no longer victims or prisoners of the past, so we can stop carrying a burden that harbors nothing but pain. As long as you say you can't forgive someone, you're spending energy against rather than being for yourself and the life you deserve. To forgive isn't giving someone permission to keep hurting you. It's not okay that you were harmed. But it's already done. No one but you can heal the wound (2020, pp. 177-178).

The difficulty of forgiveness is the topic of the next chapter. But some challenging aspects of forgiveness must be addressed in relation to the forgiver, the one confronted with this demanding work. A misconception that hinders forgiveness is that anger and forgiveness cannot coexist. Although anger is one of Christian theology's seven deadly sins, the Latin word (ire) translated as "anger" in classic texts more accurately means "rage and fury culminating in violence." Anger is an emotion and as with all emotions it comes with the responsibility to manage it. It is in this sense that the biblical teaching is, "Be ye angry and sin not" (Ephesians 4:26, KJV). Forgiveness is not an emotion, it is a commitment to think and act a certain way regardless of feelings. Another Holocaust survivor, Corrie Ten Boom, understood this and said, "Forgiveness is an act of the will, and the will can function regardless of the temperature of the heart" (2021). Forgiveness is not born of impulse, it is the product of deliberation and decision.

Forgiveness meets Aristotle's characterization of a virtue as the apex between two extremes. Forgiveness is found between the extremes of vengeance and denial. Those obsessed with getting even cannot forget; those in denial make believe they cannot remember. Forgiveness is remembering without being consumed by a desire for vengeance.

Forgiveness is a virtue that requires self-discipline. It is an act of self-discipline when someone says, "My feelings are screaming, 'Revenge!' but I choose to forgive because of the kind of person I want to be." Forgiveness is a state of mind expressed by inaction - the inaction of not taking measures outside the law to punish an offense or pursue payment for a debt. It is a state of mind resulting from the hard choice to neither resent someone nor desire misfortune for that person. Forgiveness is not forgetting. If selective amnesia were possible it would be unnecessary to forgive. Forgiveness does not result in a clean slate such that an offender's behavior has no influence on future interactions. Jesus, who unambiguously advocated forgiveness, also taught to "estimate the cost" before taking certain actions (Luke 14:28-30).

Another misconception is that forgiveness requires offenders to confess their wrongdoing. Political commentator Dennis Prager writes, "forgiveness is contingent on the sinner repenting and it can be given only by the one sinned against" (1997, p. 38). Although an appealing thought, making confessing a prerequisite to receiving forgiveness places forgiveness in the hands of the offender. Forgiveness must be entirely in the hands of the injured party. This is what Eger means with the phrases, "I have the power to free myself" and, "No one can heal the wound but you." If forgiveness is contingent upon some action by the offender then the forgiver is dependent on the one to be forgiven. This applies to the claim that the offender must ask for forgiveness. Simply stated, it doesn't seem right for the injured party to be reliant on the one who brought injury.

Oscar Wilde wryly suggested, "Always forgive your enemies, nothing annoys them so much" (2021). To the contrary, forgiveness should not be seized as an opportunity to punish the offenders by exacerbating their guilt. Another challenge is to forgive with an attitude of humility rather than moral superiority. In addition, forgiveness cannot include the impossible guarantee that the offense will never again happen. For example, what could an unfaithful spouse say or do that could provide certainty that infidelity will never again occur? Should forgiveness ever be withheld? Prager believes so and argues for this in his essay, "The Sin of Forgiveness."

> Though I am a Jew, I believe that a vibrant Christianity is essential if America's moral decline is to be reversed, and that despite theological differences, there is indeed a Judeo-Christian value system that has served as the bedrock of American civilization. For these reasons I am appalled and frightened by this feel-good doctrine of automatic forgiveness.
>
> This doctrine undermines the moral foundations of American civilization because it advances the amoral notion that no matter how much you hurt other people, millions of your fellow citizens will immediately forgive you. This doctrine destroys Christianity's central moral tenets about forgiveness--that forgiveness, even by God, is contingent on the sinner repenting, and that it can only be given to the sinner by the one against whom he sinned (1997).

Prager's position seems consistent with the teaching Jesus gave his disciples: "If your brother sins, rebuke him, and if he repents, forgive him. If he sins against you seven times in a day, and seven times comes back to you and says, 'I repent,' forgive him" (Luke 17: 3-4). The point of this hyperbolic teaching is forgiveness should never be withheld from someone who is repentant. (The hyperbole is "seven times a day.") However, this teaching does not forbid forgiving someone who has not expressed repentance. As previously stated, if repentance is a prerequisite for forgiveness then the injured party is dependent upon the offender.

The late Elie Wiesel, Holocaust survivor and Nobel laureate, said he could forgive even the concentration camp guards who abused him and killed his family if they asked to be forgiven. (He also has said he would not forgive anyone who claims the Holocaust never occurred.) In fact, he made a public appeal to Johnnes Rau, the President of Germany, to represent the German people in asking the Jewish people for their forgiveness. Speaking to the Bundestag (German parliament) on the occasion of the 55th anniversary of the liberation of the concentration camps, Wiesel concluded by urging the Bundestag to pass a resolution formally requesting,

> in the name of Germany, the forgiveness of the Jewish people for the crimes of Hitler. "Do it publicly," he said. "Ask the Jewish people to forgive Germany for what the Third Reich had done in Germany's name. Do it, and the significance of this day will acquire a higher level. Do it, for we desperately want to have hope for this new century" (Cohen, 2000).

The following month, at a private ceremony in Berlin, Rau said, "I pay tribute to all those who were subjected to slave and forced labor under German rule and, in the name of the German people, beg forgiveness" (2000).

Although a noble gesture, this raises the question of how this forgiveness is expressed. Wiesel could speak for himself as a victim and survivor, but could he forgive on behalf of six million dead people. Another survivor, Simon Wiesenthal, addresses this question in his memoir, *The Sunflower*. He describes the day he was escorted by a nurse to the hospital room of a dying German SS soldier who had requested to speak with a Jew. The soldier was so heavily bandaged that he had a mummy-like appearance. The nurse informed the soldier she had brought him the Jew he had requested and left the room.

Puzzled and afraid, Wiesenthal listened as the man in the bed recounted a horrifying story in which he participated in the killing of a number of Jews by forcing them into a building and setting it on fire. The soldier went on to explain that recently his body had been blown apart in an explosion and he soon would be dead - within a day or two. Waiting to die, the soldier was being tormented by the screams of the Jewish men, women, and children he had burned alive. He thought if Wiesenthal, a Jew, would forgive him, the screaming would stop and he could die in peace. He said, "The pains in my body are terrible, but worse still is my conscience. I know that what I am asking is almost too much for you, but without your answer I cannot die in peace." (1969, pp. 53-54).

Wiesenthal reasoned he could not forgive him because he could not speak for the people who died in that fire. He later reflected,

> Two men who had never known each other had been brought together for a few hours by Fate. One asked the other for help. But the other was himself helpless and able to do nothing for him. At last I made up my mind and without a word I left the room (p. 55).

III. Forgiving Is Difficult

The weak can never forgive. Forgiveness is an attribute of the strong.

- Mahatma Gandhi

Alexander Pope observed, "To err is human, to forgive is divine" (1711). A wry variation of Pope's observation is, "To err is human, to forgive is rare." Both allude to the difficulty of forgiving. If there are benefits derived from forgiving, as the next chapter claims, then why is it so difficult to forgive? Lynette Hoy, President of the Anger Management Institute, believes it is not in our nature to forgive:

> Human behavior suggests that people are hardwired to retaliate when they have been hurt by another person. Our pride or self-esteem is injured. Our expectations or dreams are disappointed. We lose something very valuable to us and want recompense for the damages (2021).

Psychologist Anthony Lopez agrees and writes,

> Forgiveness is difficult in part because evolution has endowed us with the psychological motivation to avoid being exploited by others, and one of the easiest ways to prevent exploitation is to hit back or simply avoid

the exploiter Therefore, any discussion of forgiveness must begin by thinking carefully about the desire for retaliation (2019).

Forgiveness in some situations goes beyond difficult to virtually inconceivable. In *How We Die*, Dr. Sherwin Nuland provides a grisly account of the murder of Katie Mason, a nine-year-old girl who died from multiple stab wounds.

> The entire grim sequence of events – hemorrhage, exsanguination, cardiac arrest, the agonal moments, clinical death, and finally irretrievable mortality – was played out during a particularly vicious murder committed a few years ago in a small Connecticut city not far from the hospital where I work. The attack took place at a crowded street fair, in full view of scores of people who had fled the scene in fear of the killer's maniacal rage. He had never laid eyes on his victim before the savage onslaught. She was a buoyant, beautiful child of nine (1995, p. 124)

The man who murdered Katie was Peter Carlquist, a psychiatric patient with paranoid schizophrenia. He had a long history of violent assaults. "As early as six he had told a psychiatrist that the devil had come up out of the ground and entered his body. Perhaps he was right" (p. 125). Shortly before his attack on Katie an advisory board at the nearby state mental hospital determined Carlquist could be trusted to sign himself out for several hours at a time.

Is it conceivable that Joan Mason, Katie's mother, could forgive Carlquist or the advisory board members who turned him loose to plunge a hunting knife repeatedly into her daughter? Who could fault Joan Mason for not forgiving Peter Carlquist? Who would insist that she should?

The story of Ronald Cotton is a story of extraordinary forgiveness. In 1984 he was identified by Jennifer Thompson-Cannino as the man who raped her. In 1995, after nearly 11 years imprisonment, he was exonerated by DNA evidence. Thompson-Cannino admitted her error and was forgiven by Cotton. In a National Public Radio interview he explained,

> Forgiving Jennifer for picking me out of that lineup as her rapist took less time than people think. I knew she was a victim and was hurting real bad. But I was hurting, too. I missed my family, my girlfriend and my freedom. But I knew who I was, and I was not that monster. I knew who did this to Jennifer, and he would have gone to his grave leaving me to rot in prison without ever confessing to what he had done. Letting go of my anger toward him was hard, but staying free in my heart was a choice only I could make (2009).

Cotton and Thompson-Cannino have co-authored a book, *Picking Cotton: A Memoir of Injustice and Redmption* (2009) in addition to speaking together at law schools and law enforcement conferences.

Christian theologian C.S. Lewis addresses the difficulty of forgiveness in his classic treatise *Mere Christianity* (1952). There he raises the hypothetical question of whether he would forgive the Gestapo if he were a Jew. He admits to not knowing if he would but adds if he ever hoped to have this capacity to forgive it would have to be developed incrementally:

> When you start mathematics you do not begin with calculus; you begin with simple addition. In the same way, if we really want (but all depends on really wanting) to learn how to forgive, perhaps we had better start with something easier than the Gestapo. One might start with forgiving one's husband or wife, or parents or children … . That will probably keep us busy for the moment (1952, p. 116).

Lewis understood the capacity for forgiveness is developmental, enlarging with practice. Shakespeare expressed this concept through Prince Hamlet, who counseled his mother, Gertrude, that with practice even difficult actions can become second nature:

> Assume a virtue, if you have it not.
> That monster, custom, who all sense doth eat,
> Of habits devil, is angel yet in this,

That to the use of actions fair and good
He likewise gives a frock or livery
That aptly is put on. Refrain tonight,
And that shall lend a kind of easiness
To the next abstinence; the next more easy;
For use almost can change the stamp of nature
(*Hamlet*, Act III, scene 4).

Why do the hard work of forgiveness?

There are at least three possible benefits for forgivers. First, the act of conforming their behavior to their personal moral code contributes to character development. Lewis said with each of life's moral decisions we make ourselves a little more a creature of heaven or a little more a creature of hell. For those who consider forgiveness a virtue each act of forgiveness makes them more the person they aspire to be. If forgiveness is seen as a virtue owing to a religious conviction then the forgiver is maturing in faith.

A second benefit is related to the first – conformity to conscience. Aristotle's formula for happiness (i.e. "overall life contentment") includes living in a manner that is consistent with one's conscience. Immanuel Kant not only emphasized the importance of conformity to conscience but has a reference to conscience written on his tombstone: "Two things fill the mind with ever new and increasing admiration and awe, the more often and steadily we reflect upon them: the starry heavens above me and the moral law within me" (2004, pp.

161-162). Conformity to conscience applies to 99 percent of the general population. In other words, 99 percent of human beings have a conscience. This means only one percent are untroubled by their behavior when it violates society's moral standards and/or brings suffering to others. (Psychologist Robert Hare, an authority on psychopaths, titled his consummate book on the subject *Without Conscience* [1999]). Forgiving is a matter of conscience for those who believe it is the right thing to do. For such people, a failure to forgive is a moral failure accompanied by the nagging voice of conscience.

A third and perhaps the greatest benefit of forgiving is the forgiver's liberation. Simply stated, not forgiving consumes a lot of psychic energy. The word resentment is derived from the French *resentir* which means "to feel again." Not forgiving results in re-experiencing pain, anger, and hatred each time the offense is replayed. Accompanying pain, anger, and hatred are plans, real or imaginary, for retribution. Not forgiving allows the offender to reside in the injured party's head without paying rent. In contrast to this bitter, self-injurious existence consider these words of Ronald Cotton:

> Jennifer and I are friends. And some people don't really understand it. But we were victims of the same injustice by the same man, and this gave us a common ground to stand on. Together we were able to help each other heal through a shared experience. I could choose to be bitter; I could hate the prison guards and the

system. But I choose to forgive them all, so that I stay free and not be a prisoner for the rest of my life (2009).

William Paul Young's bestselling novel *The Shack* is the story of a man's surreal encounter with God following his daughter's abduction and murder by a serial killer. When God tells the man, named Mack, he should forgive the murderer Mack says he is incapable of such forgiveness. God explains to him if he knew the life history of the killer he would be able to forgive him. God also tells Mack it would be good for him to forgive because his fantasies of revenge are consuming him and being pursued at the expense of the life that remains for him in spite of the catastrophic loss of his daughter.

"So what then? I just forgive him and everything is okay and we become buddies?" Mack stated softly but sarcastically.

"Forgiveness does not establish a relationship."

"I don't think I can do this," Mack answered softly.

"I want you to. Forgiveness is first for you, the forgiver," answered (God), "to release you from something that will eat you alive; that will destroy your joy and your ability to love fully and openly. As incomprehensible as it sounds at this moment, you may well know this man in a different context one day" (Young, 2007, pp. 225,227).

Theologian Lewis Smedes writes similarly in his book on forgiveness:

> Recall the pain of being wronged, the hurt of being stung, cheated, demeaned. Doesn't the memory of it fuel the fire of fury again, reheat the pain again, make it hurt again? Suppose you never forgive, suppose you feel hurt each time your memory lights on the people who did you wrong. And suppose you have a compulsion to think of them constantly. You have become a prisoner of your past pain; you are locked in a torture chamber of your own making. Time should have left your pain behind; but you keep it alive to let it flay you over and over.
>
> The only way to heal the pain that will not heal itself is to forgive the person who hurt you. Forgiving stops the reruns of pain. Forgiving heals your memory as you change you memory's vision. When you release the wrongdoer from the wrong, you cut a malignant tumor out of your life. You set a prisoner free, but you discover the real prisoner was yourself (1984, pp. 132-133).

Jesus taught, "For if you forgive other people when they sin against you, your heavenly Father will also forgive you. But if you do not forgive others their sins, your Father will not forgive your sins" (Matthew 6:14,15). Yet nowhere in their conversation does God tell Mack he must forgive in order to be forgiven. Jesus' teaching on forgiveness is the topic of chapter V. This issue is raised here because appearance to the contrary, forgiving others is not required for receiving God's forgiveness and therefore not one of the benefits of forgiving.

IV. The One to Be Forgiven

In the shadow of my hurt, forgiveness feels like a decision to reward my enemy. But in the shadow of the cross, forgiveness is merely a gift from one undeserving soul to another.

-Andy Stanley

Anyone seeking forgiveness must do so knowing that no one is entitled to forgiveness. Being forgiven is an expression of grace, which means getting something undeserved. If it is given, it is given as a gift. And while it is not owed to anyone the one to be forgiven can facilitate forgiveness by complying with certain conditions. For example, an unfaithful husband has created an atmosphere of suspicion in the relationship. Agreeing to sacrifice some privacy by allowing his wife access to his cell phone and computer is a reasonable expectation. In addition, since forgiveness is a process rather than a punctiliar event, patience is required of the husband, who must allow the pace of forgiveness to be set by his wife. Moreover, his patience will be tested by questions, often repetitive, as well times when his wife will be silent or sad, which will appear to be relapses into unforgiveness. In forgiveness the feelings of the injured party take precedence over the feelings of the one who brought injury. Finally, even when forgiveness is presented as unconditional the one forgiven has the implicit obligation to take opportunities to "pay it forward" by forgiving others.

As previously stated, forgiveness doesn't require the offender to ask for it or demonstrate repentance. This would make the forgiver dependent on the one to be forgiven. This being said, the one seeking forgiveness can facilitate it by unambiguously taking responsibility and expressing remorse. Albert Speer, part of Adolf Hitler's inner circle and convicted as a Nazi war criminal at Nuremberg, expressed remorse and took responsibility for his contribution to the Holocaust. In a letter to Simon Wiesenthal, a Holocaust survivor, following his visit to Speer, he writes,

> Even after twenty years of imprisonment at Spandau, I can never forgive myself for recklessly and unscrupulously supporting a regime that carried out the systematic murder of Jews and other groups of people. My moral guilt is not subject to the statute of limitations, it cannot be erased in my lifetime. Every human being has his burden to bear. No one can remove it for another, but for me, ever since that day, it has become much lighter. It is God's grace that has touched me through you (Wiesenthal, 1969, pp. 245, 246).

Forgiving Ourselves

In self-forgiving the receiver is also the giver. In contrast to Speer is boxing legend Muhammed Ali. In his forties, reflecting on the philandering of his youth, he expressed remorse and self-forgiveness:

> I used to chase women all the time. And I won't say it was right, but look at all the temptations I had. I was young, handsome, heavyweight champion of the world. Women were always offering themselves to me. I had two children by women I wasn't married to. I love them; they're my children. I feel just as good and proud of them as I do my other children, but it wasn't the right thing to do. And running around, living that kind of life, wasn't good for me. It hurt my wife, it offended God. It never really made me happy. But ask any man who's forty years old – if he knew at twenty what he knows now, would he do things different? Most people would. So I did wrong; I'm sorry. And all I'll say as far as running around chasing women is concerned, is that's all past. I've got a good wife now, and I'm lucky to have her (1991, p. 310).

If he seems to be too easy on himself, why? Would another decade or two of living with self-recrimination make his remorse more sincere? Would self-flagellation make his regret more believable? Jesus taught to "love your neighbor as yourself" (Matthew 22:39). C.S. Lewis said this means loving others in the same way we love ourselves and writes, "I admit that this means loving people who have nothing lovable about them. But then, has oneself anything lovable about it? You love it simply because it is yourself" (1952, p. 120). Usually, when we've misbehaved we feel guilty but eventually we forgive ourselves. This is the way in which we love ourselves. The principles that apply to forgiving others also apply to self-forgiveness and vice versa.

V. Jesus' Teaching on Forgiveness

Bear with each other and forgive one another if any of you has a grievance against someone. Forgive as the Lord forgave you.

- Colossians 3:13

Thomas Erskine, Lord Chancellor to King George III, observed, "In the New Testament religion is grace and ethics is gratitude" (2021). Grace is unmerited favor; to be the recipient of grace is to receive something unearned and undeserved. As previously stated, no one is entitled to forgiveness, making it an expression of grace. Gratitude is the appropriate response to forgiveness, hence the implicit obligation to forgive others. All of the above is present in Jesus' teaching on forgiveness. Forgiveness is essential to the Christian faith. (This chapter has relevance only for Christians or those who are curious about what Jesus taught about forgiveness.)

There is a challenge to understanding Jesus' teaching on forgiveness. Statements like, "forgive us our debts, as we also have forgiven our debtors" (Matthew 6:12) and, "if you do not forgive others their sins, your father will not forgive your sins" (Matthew 6:15) seem to make God's forgiveness contingent on sinners forgiving other sinners. This was C.S. Lewis' understanding of "this terrible duty of forgiving" (1952, p.115). In *Mere Christianity* he writes:

Just as when Christianity tells me I must not deny my religion even to save myself from death and torture, I wonder very much what I should do when it came to the point. I am not trying to tell you in this book what I could do – I can do precious little – I am telling you what Christianity is. I did not invent it. And there, right in the middle of it, I find "Forgive us our sins as we forgive those that sin against us." There is no slightest suggestion we are offered forgiveness on any other terms. It is made perfectly clear that if we do not forgive we shall not be forgiven. There are no two ways about it (pp. 115-116).

The problem with this understanding is that it makes God's forgiveness conditional and subject to revocation. If God's forgiveness was fully accomplished with the crucifixion of Jesus then no additional work is required for forgiveness and salvation. To require sinners to forgive others in order to secure their salvation is to reduce Christ's sacrificial death to necessary but insufficient for entrance into the kingdom of God. This assertion is contrary to the Apostle Paul's emphatic declaration: "For it is by grace you have been saved, through faith – and this is not from yourselves, it is the gift of God – not by works, so that no one can boast" (Ephesians 2:8-9).

The way out of this conundrum is to understand the biblical teaching is not that sinners must forgive in order to acquire and maintain their salvation. Rather, forgiving others is part of the Christian life. Professing Christians who withhold forgiveness are demonstrating a lack of gratitude for the forgiveness they have received, calling into question the sincerity of their faith. Moreover, their unwillingness to forgive (or at least strive to forgive) demonstrates a failure to understand God's forgiveness. Citizenship in the kingdom of God includes "paying forward" forgiveness as well as not keeping a record of offenses. Christians who eschew forgiving others are implying a preference for punishment and/or recompense for their sins. This preference is incompatible with citizenship in God's kingdom. Anyone who has received forgiveness and withholds it from others is characterized by the unmerciful servant described in a parable told by Jesus:

> "Therefore, the kingdom of heaven is like a king who wanted to settle accounts with his servants. As he began the settlement, a man who owed him ten thousand bags of gold was brought to him. Since he was not able to pay, the master ordered that he and his wife and his children and all that he had be sold to repay the debt.
>
> "The servant fell on his knees before him. 'Be patient with me,' he begged 'and I will pay back everything.' The servant's master took pity on him, canceled the debt and let him go.
>
> "But when that servant went out, he found one of his fellow servants who owed him a hundred denarii. He grabbed him and began to choke him. 'Pay back what you owe me!' he demanded.

"His fellow servant fell to his knees and begged him, 'Be patient with me, and I will pay you back.' "But he refused. Instead, he went off and had the man thrown into prison until he could pay the debt. When the other servants saw what had happened, they were greatly distressed and went and told their master everything that had happened.

"Then the master called the servant in. 'You wicked servant,' he said, 'I canceled all that debt of yours because you begged me to. Shouldn't you have had mercy on your fellow servant just as I had on you?' In anger his master handed him over to the jailers to be tortured, until he should pay back all he owed.

"This is how my heavenly Father will treat each of you unless you forgive your brother from your heart" (Matthew 18:23-35).

Clearly, the message conveyed in this parable is a failure to forgive others after having been forgiven is egregious misconduct. The point is emphasized by the use of hyperbole. The debt owed by the unmerciful servant is 600,000 times greater than the debt owed to him. The master forgave a debt equal to the wages for 200,000 years of labor while the unmerciful servant refused to forgive a debt equal to one day's wages. The last verse of the parable expresses the master's anger toward the servant and the action taken by the master. In essence, the master says to him, "Since you prefer punishment and repayment to forgiveness then punishment and repayment will be required of you." The benefit of the master's forgiveness came with the expectation that the servant would extend forgiveness to his debtors. An unwillingness to forgive or even try to forgive is conduct unbecoming a Christian and, as stated above, calls into question a profession of faith. By analogy, a citizen of the United States who doesn't vote, pay taxes, obey laws or respect the flag and regards the Constitution with contempt is nominally American. But such conduct calls into question the sincerity of any claim to being an American.

Hyperbole abounds in Jesus' teaching on forgiveness. When asked by Peter how many times he should forgive, Peter suggested seven as the maximum number. Jesus countered with "not seven but seventy-seven times" (Matthew 18:22). With this response Jesus was not raising the limit by seventy but instructing Peter the number of times a person asks for forgiveness is the number of times it should be given. The principle conveyed by this purposeful exaggeration is to forgive, not count.

Also hyperbolic is Jesus' teaching that forgiveness should be extended even if an offender sins and repents multiple times in the same day: "Even if they sin against you seven times in a day and seven times come back to you saying 'I repent,' you must forgive them" (Luke 17:4). Of course, anyone who would offend the same person seven times in one day is amoral and unlikely to apologize even once, let alone seven times. Implicit in this teaching is judgment and punishment will be administered eventually by God.

Understandably, this was another occasion for his disciples to say, "This is a hard teaching. Who can accept it?" (John 6:60).

In all of this it's important to note that forgiving does not mean maintaining or resuming a relationship with an offender oblivious to his history. As stated in the first chapter, Jesus also taught to "estimate the cost" before taking a significant action (Luke 14:28). Nowhere in scripture is it taught that believers have an obligation to make themselves available for mistreatment.

Among theologians and New Testament scholars is a long-running discussion of the meaning of one of the seven recorded statements made by Jesus while being crucified. The statement, "Father forgive them, for they do not know what they are doing" (Luke 23:34) raises the question of to whom "them" refers. Was Jesus interceding for the Roman soldiers carrying out his execution, the Jewish ruling council that betrayed him, the jeering crowd that witnessed his crucifixion or all of humankind? In turn, this raises another question: For each possibility, what did they not know? Most of them did not know they had a part in putting God incarnate to death. Although it should be noted that Jesus once antagonized a group of his critics by saying, "I and the Father are one" (John 10:30) and that he should be accepted as a messenger sent by God, if not God himself:

> Jesus said to them, "I have shown you many great miracles from the Father. For which of these do you stone me?"

"We are not stoning you for any of these," replied the Jews, "but for blasphemy, because you, a mere man, claim to be God" (John 10:32-33).

Perhaps Jesus had the Roman soldiers in mind when he said they didn't know what they were doing. They had no reason to suspect they were putting to death an innocent man. To them the crucifixion of Jesus was merely the execution of another criminal. The same can be said about those in the crowd who taunted Jesus, believing he was a false messiah. As for all of humankind, a well-known Christian hymn has the refrain,

> He was nailed to the cross for me,
> He was nailed to the cross for me,
> On the cross crucified for me he died,
> He was nailed to the cross for me (Graves, 1906).

As the savior of humankind perhaps Jesus interceded for the generations of sinners – past, present, and future – whose transgressions were responsible for his calling as the sacrificial lamb of God. Most people throughout the ages do not see themselves as responsible for the death of Jesus. And when blame is so widely distributed it is unlikely any individual will take fault. As several writers have observed, no snowflake in an avalanche ever feels responsible.

Whoever Jesus had in mind when he prayed for their forgiveness, their ignorance was the rationale for his intercession. Ignorance on the part of the sinner facilitates forgiveness. Even a child can understand this, as did six-year-old Ruby Bridges. In 1960 she was the first black child to attend a previously all-white elementary school in New Orleans, Louisiana. Her safety required her to be escorted by federal marshals. In an interview with child psychiatrist Robert Coles he asked her what she was thinking when threatened and harassed by a protesting mob as she entered the school. She told him, "I was talking to God." Coles then asked her what she was saying to God. She replied, "Father, try to forgive these people because they don't know what they're doing" (Coles, 2007).

Forgiveness and Divorce

When responding to a question concerning divorce Jesus simultaneously provided a teaching on forgiveness:

> Some Pharisees came to him to test him. They asked, "Is it lawful for a man to divorce his wife for any and every reason?"
>
> "Haven't you read," he replied, "that at the beginning the Creator 'made them male and female,' and said, 'For this reason a man will leave his father and mother and be united to his wife, and the two will become one flesh.' So they are no longer two, but one. Therefore what God has joined together, let man not separate."

"Why then," they asked, "did Moses command that a man give his wife a certificate of divorce and send her away?"

Jesus replied, "Moses permitted you to divorce your wives because your hearts were hard. But it was not this way from the beginning. I tell you that anyone who divorces his wife, except for marital unfaithfulness, and marries another woman commits adultery" (Matthew 19:3-9).

Although the word "forgive" does not appear in this narrative, it is implied that it is better to divorce than live with a betrayed spouse who cannot forgive. It is God's preference that when a marriage is contaminated by adultery the unfaithful spouse repents and the betrayed spouse forgives. However, Jesus added, if forgiveness is beyond the capability of the injured party then although divorce is undesirable it is the lesser of two evils when compared to life with someone who cannot forgive. (Jesus expressed no condemnation of a betrayed spouse who could not forgive.)

The Unpardonable Sin

Surprisingly, Jesus taught there is a sin for which there is no forgiveness from God. Referred to as, "blasphemy of the Holy Spirit," it places a sinner beyond the reach of God, who would forgive if he could:

Then they brought him a demon-possessed man who was blind and mute, and Jesus healed him, so that he could both talk and see. All the people were astonished and said, "Could this be the Son of David?"

But when the Pharisees heard this, they said, "It is only by Beelzebub, the prince of demons, that this fellow drives out demons."

Jesus knew their thoughts and said to them, "Every kingdom divided against itself will be ruined, and every city or household divided against itself will not stand.

"If Satan drives out Satan, he is divided against himself. How then can his kingdom stand? And if I drive out demons by Beelzebub, by whom do your people drive them out? So then, they will be your judges. But if I drive out demons by the Spirit of God, then the kingdom of God has come upon you. Or again, how can anyone enter a strong man's house and carry off his possessions unless he first ties up the strong man? Then he can plunder his house.

"He who is not with me is against me, and whoever does not gather with me scatters. And so I tell you, every sin and blasphemy will be forgiven men, but the blasphemy against the Spirit will not be forgiven. Anyone who speaks a word against the Son of Man will be forgiven, but anyone who speaks against the Holy Spirit will not be forgiven, either in this age or in the age to come" (Matthew 12: 22-32).

What does it mean to speak against the Holy Spirit and why is it unforgivable to do so? An analogy might be helpful in understanding the answer to both questions. Suppose I said to you, "I'll have something very important to tell you tomorrow and the only way I'll have to reach you is the telephone. When you see my number on your cell phone make sure you take my call. Remember, this is the only way I'll be able to reach you." Further imagine that when I make the call you refuse to take it, insisting, "If he wants to talk to me it'll have to be in person, not over the phone." Having rejected the only means for reaching you, the important message is never delivered.

In the gospel narrative quoted above Jesus tells the Pharisees that God has determined to communicate an important message to them by way of miracles with the Holy Spirit bearing witness that they are seeing God at work. The Holy Spirit stirred within them to confirm that they have seen God at work through Jesus. Instead, the Pharisees defied this verification and constructed the illogical, indefensible explanation that Beelzebub, the prince of demons, is the source of Jesus' power. Jesus concludes the confrontation by telling them they have resisted the only means by which God will reach them, thereby placing themselves beyond God's forgiveness.

References

Chapter I.

Barnicle, M. (2021). Recovered from https://brainyquote.com on 05/17/2021.

Farrar, E. (1997). Letters of a nation. A collection of American letters. Andrew Carroll, Editor. New York: Broadway Books.

Griswald, C. (2007). Forgiveness: A philosophical exploration. New York: Cambridge University Press.

Luskin, F. (2002). Forgive for good: A proven prescription for health and happiness. New York: HarperCollins Publishers.

Martin, Mike W. (1989). Everyday morality: An introduction to applied ethics. Belmont, CA. Wadsworth Publishing Co., 1989).

Chapter II.

Cohen, R. (2000). "Wiesel urges Germany to ask forgiveness." The New York Times. 01/28/2000.

Eger, E. (2020). The gift: 12 lessons to save your life. New York: Scribner. Ten Boom, C. (2021).

Prager, D. (1997). "The sin of forgivenss." The Wall Street Journal. 12/15/1997.

Wiesenthal, S. (1969). The sunflower: On the possibilities and limits of forgiveness. New York: Schoecken Books Inc.

Wilde, O. (2021). Recovered from brainyquote.com/ quotes/oscar_wilde_10522 on 06/08/2021.

Chapter III

Cotton, R. (2005). "All things considered." National Public Radio. 03/05/2009.

Cotton, R. and Thompson-Cannino, J. with Erin Torneo. (2009). Picking Cotton: A memoir of injustice and redemption. New York: St. Martin's Griffin.

Hoy, L. (2020). "Why is it so hard to forgive?" Recovered from "Issues I face" website on 06/10/2021.

Kant, I. (2004). *Critique of pure reason*. Thomas K. Abbott (translator). Mineola, NY: Dover Philosophical Classics.

Lewis, C.S. (1952). Mere Christianity. New York: HarperCollins Publishers.

Lopez, A. (2019). "Why is it so hard to forgive?" Psychology today website. Posted 04/01/2019.

Nuland, S. (1995). How we die: Reflections on life's final chapter. New York: Random House.

Pope, A. (1711). An essay on criticism. Recovered from The Poetry Foundation. Chicago, IL.

Smedes, L. (1984). Forgive and forget: Healing the hurts we don't deserve. San Francisco, CA: Harper & Row Publishers.

Young, W.P. (2007). The shack. Los Angeles, CA: Windblown Media.

Chapter IV

Hare, R. (1999). Without conscience: The disturbing world of psychopaths among us. New York: Guilford Press.

Hauser, T. (1991). Muhammed Ali: His life and times. New York: Simon and Schuster.\

Lewis, C.S. (1952). Mere Christianity. New York: HarperCollins Publishers.

Wiesenthal, S. (1969). The sunflower: On the possibilities and limits of forgiveness. New York: Schoecken Books Inc.

Chapter V

Coles, R. (2007). Listening to children: A moral journey with Robert Coles. PBS Home Video.

Erskine, T. (2021). thomas_erskine_184402 on 06/26/2021.

Graves, F.A. (1906). "He was nailed to the cross for me." Public Domain.

Lewis, C.S. (1952). Mere christianity. New York: HarperCollins Publishers.

About the Author

Max Malikow brings 35 years of teaching philosophy to the subject of forgiveness. He earned a Bachelor's degree from the University of Nebraska, Master's degree from Gordon-Conwell Theological Seminary, and doctorate from Boston University. He is on the faculty of the Renee Crown Honors Program of Syracuse University and an Adjunct Professor of Philosophy at LeMoyne College. The author or editor of 19 previous books, he is a practicing psychotherapist in Syracuse, New York.

Other Books by Max Malikow

Why Is Life So Difficult? Reflections and Suggestions.

Six Paths to a Good Life

Heroism and Virtue: Reflections on Human Greatness

Buried Above Ground: Understanding Suicide and the Suicidal Mind

Christ the Counselor: Reflecting on Jesus as a Therapist.

It Happened in Little Valley: A Case Study of Uxoricide

Death: Reflections on the End of Life and What Comes After.

Mere Existentialism: A Primer

It's Not Too Late! Making the Most of the Rest of Your Life (third edition)

The Human Predicament: Towards an Understanding of the Human Situation

Philosophy Reader: Essays and Articles for Thought and Discussion

Being Human: Philosophical Reflections on Psychological Issues

Philosophy 101: A Primer for the Apathetic or Struggling Student

Suicidal Thoughts: Essays on Self-Determined Death

Profiles in Character: Twenty-Six Stories that Will Instruct and Inspire Teenagers

Teachers for Life: Advice and Methods Gathered Along the Way

What Is Philosophy and Why Study It? The Case for Relevance

Living When a Young Friend Commits Suicide: Or Is Even Thinking About It (co-authored with Rabbi Dr. Earl A. Grollman)

Why Be Good? And Other Questions Concerning Moral Philosohy

Made in the USA
Middletown, DE
23 December 2021